Schirmer's Visual Library 15
Frida Kahlo — Masterpieces

The Mexican painter Frida Kahlo (1907—1954) was first discovered in Europe in the early 1980s. Since then, interest in her strongly autobiographical work has been constantly growing.

Her fascinating, colorful paintings reflect her own unhappy personal history, her relationship with the painter Diego Rivera, her physical condition, her philosophy of nature and life, and her individual and mythological worldview—which would have been inconceivable without the revival of Indian culture in the Mexico of her time. "She is the first woman in the history of art who took up, with absolute and ruthless sincerity, themes that exclusively concern women," wrote Diego Rivera about his wife, who emancipated herself in painting through the sheer force of her personality. Her small-format works, however, are more than merely documents of one woman's liberation; they sum up in artistic terms Frida Kahlo's own story in the context of the collective reality of Mexican history. Forty-three selected masterpieces illustrate here how Frida Kahlo developed to become the great Mexican painter who fascinated André Breton, Picasso, and Eisenstein during her own lifetime, and who today enjoys worldwide recognition. The introduction is by the german writer Keto von Waberer.

112 pages, 43 color plates

Frida Kahlo in her studio, ca. 1945

Frida Kahlo

Masterpieces

Introduction by
Keto von Waberer

W. W. Norton
New York   London

Cover painting:
Self-portrait with Monkeys, 1943
Oil on canvas, 81.5 x 63 cm (32 x 25 in.)
Gelman Collection, Mexico

Translation from the German by Michael Robertson

The reproduction of works by Frida Kahlo is by kind permission of the Instituto Nacional
de Bellas Artes, Mexico City.

© for this edition 1994 by Schirmer / Mosel GmbH, Munich

Reproductions: O. R. T. Kirchner GmbH, Berlin
Composition: Gerber Satz GmbH, München
Printed and bound in Germany

ISBN 0-393-31257-7

A Schirmer / Mosel Production
Published by W. W. Norton & Company
New York · London

Contents

Keto von Waberer

"Nothing is black, really nothing."

When I first saw Frida Kahlo's eyes, she was looking down at me from a wall. A small, very colorful painting, hanging among many other paintings. She was looking at me, looking into my eyes, and I felt her watching me, the whole evening long, wherever I went in the large, bright room, among the talking, laughing people.

That was many years ago in a house in Pedregal, a villa suburb of Mexico City, where solidified lava fields ran up to the edge of the road and right up to the walls of the gardens, and where the flowering plants and the fountains turned the gardens into miracles.

I was to see this hard, inhuman landscape and luxuriant vegetation again later, in some of her paintings. I would like to be able to say that Frida's face—framed by a monkey and a cat, and with a dead humming-bird that followed the line of her eyebrows with the shape of its wings— haunted me after that evening; but it would not be true.

Her expressions as she looked at me disturbed me and confused me, even annoyed me. Her face seemed beautiful and horrifying at the same time, serious and expressionless, her glance unwavering. She knew something and was not telling me what it was. It was a message, I understood that much, but at the time I could not decode it and did not even want to receive it—yet. I decided to forget the strange painting. Nor did I ask about Frida Kahlo, although I know now that I would have been able to find out about her from the people who were there, all of whom were older than I and knew her personally.

The time Frida lived in, which is not actually all that long ago, seemed to me then to be as far away as the Middle Ages. For a European, time in

7

Mexico becomes strangely distorted, since the criteria one normally uses to measure the course of development—the evidence of art , architecture, furniture, and accessories—are lacking. But Frida's art can be understood only when one looks at historical events and at the roots from which the contemporary flowering of Mexican painting, poetry, and folk art grew.

Married to the painter Diego Riviera, Frida lived at the center of events. It was a period of cultural renewal, more a philosophical than a political renewal. The so-called Mexican renaissance, on which Rivera himself had the most formative influence, cannot of course be compared to the European one—in Italy, for example. The revolution that had taken place in the preceding years, even before the Russian Revolution, was also a different, entirely Mexican affair. There was no revolutionary Marxist or socialist theory here. The Communist Party was formed only after the revolution. Zapata hoped for a return to the pre-Columbian form of land distribution and the Aztec form of village organization, for a resurrection of a period that is much less distant in the past for Mexico than the period of the Romans and Greeks is for Europeans. When one realizes that Tenochtitlán, the forerunner of Mexico City, was founded by the Aztecs in the thirteenth century and destroyed at the beginning of the sixteenth, one can see why Rivera was influenced in his mural painting by Giotto, Piero, and Mantegna. The Aztec era coincides with the flowering of the Renaissance in Italy, and the Aztec language, Nahuatl, was still spoken by large parts of the population afer the revolution. Rivera, who during the revolution made his artistic breakthrough in Europe, returned from Paris to Mexico with ideological and political goals, to stengthen and continue the revolution through his monumental murals. His gigantic frescoes, linking the painting of historical scenes with Mexican folk art, and cubism with pre-Columbian art, show how important for him and his time the strong national sentiment that developed during the revolution was; and it was not only the intellectuals but primarily the people themselves who were to share in this feeling. His frescoes are gigantic comic strips in which even the illiterate could read about the history of the Mexican people. Rivera was a Latin American Communist. Frida, too, had joined the party while she was still in high school. She lived in an atmosphere of upheaval, in a powerful new era in which her friends and comrades competed with one another to achieve self-realization and to explore their cultural roots through art.

Compared with the monumentality of Diego's immense frescoes, Frida's work is small in format, but it addressed the same concerns with which her husband and her period were so passionately involved. She did this in her own way. She lived in the shadow of a painter and ideologist, but never measured herself against him. His influence in her work is visible, but her influence on his art, an influence that is much more subtle, can also be recognized. Having personally experienced the end of the violent revolution herself, she still firmly believed in the necessity of changing social and political structures in Mexico. Her nationalist and anti-imperialist views shape her paintings' message.

Rivera encouraged his wife to paint—she had begun to paint before she met him, and brought her paintings to his studio for his comments —and he admired her paintings and recognized them for what they were, what Breton later described as "ribbons round a bomb." "Frida is a unique example in the history of art of someone tearing open her breast and heart to state the biological truth and what it feels like," Rivera wrote, describing her as "the most important painter, one who provides the best evidence of a renaissance in Mexican painting." In the only letter he ever wrote to Rivera, Picasso declared, "Neither Derain, nor you, nor I can paint a head in the way Frida Kahlo does."

Every personality is political. When Frida dealt with social questions, she always did so through an examination of a private problem. She made herself the principal theme of her own art, in which she manifested her inner experiences, dreams, fantasies, fears, and hopes. It is not she herself and her sufferings that are in the foreground, however, but a recognition that her condition is generally valid and symbolic of the suffering of all humanity, and must be seen in this way if one is not to evade the spiritual growth deriving from it. Looking at her life, one might say that she had no choice but to conjure up suffering in her painting, to exorcise it, and to make it bearable. One could also say that the arbitrary moment that brought about the change in her life opened up for her a door to fields into which no one had yet penetrated in art. She became a chronicler, researcher, and revolutionary, a traveler in the landscape full of dread that she bears witness to in her paintings. And she achieved this by using as her stylistic tool a powerful language that she chose for herself and developed further to produce a magical alphabet. It is difficult to resist her message. All of us conceal within ourselves the realm into which she was cast. What she brings to us from it touches our souls with painful recognition, with fear, with hope and triumph. What Frida says affects us all. She spreads her life out before us, and as long as she holds us in her spell, it becomes our own life. "The essential moment of a person's spiritual development is the education of the emotions. If there is any social force that has emotion as its content, it is the work of art," Raquel Tibol noted in her book about the painter.

Frida Kahlo was born on July 6, 1907, in her parents' house in Coyoacán, a suburb of Mexico City. Her father, a photographer, the son of Hungarian Jews from the German town of Baden-Baden, had married her mother, who was of Indian and Spanish extraction, in Mexico. Shortly afterward, they traveled together throughout the country, to photograph the ruins of Aztec temples. Frida, who as a child contracted polio, which left her right leg permanently weakened, suffered a serious accident at the age of eighteen that changed her life. The school bus she was traveling in was rammed by a streetcar, and a piece of iron tore into her pelvis and back. She would struggle with the effects of this accident and the pain it caused for the rest of her life. During the time she had to spend in hospital, she began to draw and paint. She joined the Communist Party and, through the photographer Tina Modotti, met Diego Rivera, whose paintings she had admired since she was a girl. They were married in 1929. Frida was twenty-two and Diego forty-two. After ten years of marriage, they became divorced, following a long separation, but they later remarried. They both had extramarital love affairs, some of Frida's being with women, but she found Diego's violent love affairs, including one with her younger sister, more and more difficult to bear. Diego and Frida were nevertheless famous as a couple. They formed the focus of an intellectual circle, and their Blue House, where they lived,

Frida and Diego, ca. 1954

attracted visitors and like-minded people from all over the world. Trotsky, too, spent some of his period of exile in their house.

During the early part of their marriage, Frida accompanied Diego on many journeys to America, but later she could no longer manage this. All her life she suffered from the injuries caused by the accident. She had to wear plaster jackets, underwent countless operations, and was often confined to bed for months on end. She was in constant pain. Against her doctors' advice, she tried to have a child, and suffered repeated miscarriages. Her illness meant that she was more and more noticeably thrown back on her own resources, and she was forced to withdraw more and more into an inner, private sphere. She painted obsessively and uninterruptedly, often while lying in bed or while hospitalized. To begin with, she gave her paintings away to friends, with no thought of selling them. André Breton, who visited her in 1938, "recognized" her as a surrealist, a label she did not agree to. "I paint my reality," she said. Breton nevertheless arranged for her first exhibition in New York in 1939 with Julien Levy, which was an immense success. During the 1940s, she taught students, who became known as Los Fridos. In the 1950s, her health increasingly deteriorated. In 1953, one of her legs had to be amputated. She died in 1954. The last photograph of her shows her in a wheelchair at a demonstration against CIA interference in the Guatemalan presidential election.

The Blue House, in which she spent most of her life, is now the Frida Kahlo Museum. Alongside paintings and drawings, the house contains many of the objects she collected and displayed around her, things she lived with. These include her famous collection of votive and ex-voto pictures, Mexican toys made of tin, papier-mâché, pumpkins, ceramics, and wire, decorated sugar-beet skulls produced for the Sunday before Advent (Commemoration of the Dead), life-sized "Judas Dolls" made of reeds or paper that are burned at Easter, mirrors and picture frames made of thin metal foil, paper flags and colorful garlands used for decorating the street during festivals, and piñatas—life-sized animals and monsters that are dangled on a string above the children at Christmas and rain down candies when they burst open.

"In Mexico, genuine art is folk art," wrote Diego. "It is made by individuals from the people for the people, it is not imposed from above, it is not sophisticated, and it is much more advanced than the painters of the various schools, with all their experiments."

In the kitchen of the house stands the clay pottery that is still on sale in the markets and widely used, the shallow stoneware tubs in which tortilla dough is kneaded, the pestles and mortars made of porous lava stone in which chilis are crushed. Rivera's splendid collection of pre-Columbian figures is now unfortunately housed in other museums. As friends of the family describe it, even then the juicy, thick-leaved plants typical of Mexico were rampant in the garden. All of these things can be seen in Frida's paintings. The animals, too, which populate her self-portraits and allegories, lived in the Blue House at the time, and their photographs remain on display. The tame spider monkeys, the roebuck called Granizo, the hairless dog called Señor Xólotl, which Frida loved, and the parrots, caterpillars, and beetles.

Frida with a pre-Columbian sculpture, ca. 1925

Frida lived in this cosmos of her own creation very much as a part of it. She wore Mexican folk costume and pre-Columbian jewelry, and combed her hair to match, adorning it with ribbons and scarves. Even when she was in the United States, she wore this Indian "masquerade," which Rivera liked to see her in, and she was amused to find herself influencing American fashion and appearing in *Vogue*. But even this disguise, and the eccentricity associated with it, was part of her artistic and political message. She stylized herself and her surroundings in the same way she stylized the still lifes, plants, and objects in her paintings, made them symbols of an attitude to life, and created a world in which to embed herself and her private story. Breton, who was enchanted both by Frida and by her art, describes her as a "fairy-tale princess with magical powers . . . in a dress made of gilded butterfly wings."

In her work, Frida questioned the purity of art and thus the established artistic tradition. Many important Mexican artists of the time celebrated the high quality of folk art production, but none of them incorporated it into their work as consistently as Frida Kahlo did. She used the art forms of her people as a means of conjuring up the mythical past that forms a bond between the whole people of Mexico. A wide variety of elements are fused together in her work. The clearest influence is that of ex-voto and votive pictures—small paintings on sheet zinc that are stuck to the walls of churches as tokens of thanksgiving or as prayers for favors. They show images of horrifying accidents and diseases and are inscribed with prayers and precise descriptions of difficult situations. Frida used these forms and combined them with references to the colonial Catholic church, religious pictures, and displays of instruments of torture, the classic emblems of pain and suffering.

Naive murals from tequila joints in the poorer areas were assimilated at the time by many artists, and Frida, too, was stimulated by them. During the last years of her life, she and her students painted pulqueria taverns.

Her paintings take up the tradition of historical portrait painting, but break out of it again through their use of Indian symbolism. She tells stories of the sort familiar from the posters displayed by street-ballad singers at fairgrounds. Her use of irony resembles that of her contemporary Posada, who in his laconic drawings depicted everyday street violence. Like folk art painters, she is little concerned in her paintings with proportion and perspective, and devotes loving attention to even the tiniest details. Many of Frida's paintings are self-portraits or at least tell her own story; no one else in the history of art ever produced self-portraits like these. Never before in the history of art had the artist's own person, her story, and her feelings been presented, and lived through, in such a complex way. It is a discovery of Frida Kahlo's.

In 1982, the Whitechapel Gallery in London put on a retrospective of Frida Kahlo's work that was a resounding success. She was rediscovered, and quickly became a cult figure. Some of the ideologies she was held up as representing resulted in false interpretations of her work. But all of this has led to the enormous popularity she enjoys today. She is better known in Europe than many other Mexican painters.

She has been called a painter of pain. But I cannot see her in this way, because it would constrict her work and reduce it. Her paintings are

14

triumphant affirmations of life, of pleasure, of fertility, of eroticism and sensuality. She changed the term *naturaleza muerta* (the Spanish for still life—"dead nature") to *naturaleza viva*. Her plants and fruit have the appearance of breathing creatures, living beings, and sexual organs. Her colors, her splendid costumes and accessories, the extravagant, juicy plants and flowers among which her figures are placed—all of these seem to be trembling with boisterous life. Even when they are describing pain, her self-portraits are always full of vitality and free from any sort of resignation. She may excite horror, but never pity. She never identified with pain or turned to the observer of the painting to appeal for sympathy. She saw herself as a symbol of pain, and her concern was to understand suffering. She instrumentalized pain. Death, which is lurking in all her paintings, should be seen not only from the point of view of Aztec tradition, in which it was seen as an inescapable part of life—a goddess like Coatlicue had equal dominion over life and death. With its constant presence in our lives, death is also what makes each instant of our lives unique and worth living.

Her painting has been described as a form of therapy, as her way of dealing with pain and maintaining control over her ravaged body. But it seems to me that, through the pain she suffered throughout her life, and through her resulting fixation on her own body, she was able to go far beyond this type of self-therapy. She was able to open a door into herself, and what she could see and understand of what lay beyond it is—apart from her own personal story—a generally valid discovery about the fragility and cruelty of the human situation as such. By transforming this condition into a symbolic form, she allows us to share in her life's struggle. Her paintings are like windows onto our secret inner world, in which it is not merely a matter of the suffering of one woman. The old division of roles that assigns the inner sphere to woman and the external one to man—whether in the home, in the body, or in the soul—is undermined by Frida Kahlo through what she reveals of this sphere. She robs inner space of its traditional image as a place of refuge. She destroys the comforting vision of a withdrawal to the womb, of woman as a source of security.

Frida wearing a plaster jacket on which
she has painted a hammer and sickle,
ca. 1950

Her self-portraits, her disguises, and the naturalness with which she showed and painted her disfiguring plaster jacket and displayed her wounds make it clear that she did not want to be seen only as a woman. She never shows any shyness or cruelty. She forces us to understand her as a human being, as a human being living out her own narcissism obsessively and with pleasure and insisting, as Frida, as a triumphant martyr, on being a generally valid symbol for us all: someone who accepts her fate, challenges it, defeats it again and again, and reports on the struggle as in a heroic epic. The sense of horror her paintings often produce results from her exposing and touching a deeply human nerve: the fact that we are fragile and mortal, that we become real human beings only when we grasp this, that we are genuinely alive only when we accept it, and that we can reach this discovery only through suffering. "Everything is and moves according to a single law: life," she wrote. "No one is different from anyone. No one fights for himself or herself alone. Everything is all and one. Fear and pain and desire and death are all part of existence."

Frida was not a surrealist, since she refused to separate reality from fantasies. She dissolved the distinction between the internal and the external worlds, the distinction between body and soul, between what happens and what one feels. Her creative power always derived from the imagination, from the fears, hopes, and absurdities of her own story, which—not without a certain ironical bitterness—she shaped into the scenes and stories that are her message to us. She allows us to share in the processes involved in her various conditions, in their causes and effects. In each self-portrait, she shows us a fresh aspect of this metamorphosis. None of them is the same as another. In this way, she succeeds in showing something that cannot really be shown: the power of the imagination. That is her unique gift.

Plates

This first self-portrait was made in 1926. She painted it for her friend Alejandro, who was angry with her for being unfaithful. Like all the later self-portraits, it conjures up affection and attentiveness. "I beg you to hang it [the painting] somewhere low down, where you will be able to look at me," she told him.

1 Self-Portrait in Silk Dress 1926

Oil on canvas, 79.9 x 59.5 cm (31½ x 23½ in.)
Private collection, Mexico City

She finished this wedding portrait only two years after they were married. It is in the style of naive portraits of the nineteenth century. As was usual in such paintings, the bird carries a banner with information. The banner can also be understood as a slight wink from Frida, who is presenting herself as a little doll whose useless feet hardly touch the ground: "Here you see us, me , Frida Kahlo, with my beloved husband, Diego Rivera."

2 Frida and Diego Rivera 1931

Oil on canvas, 100 x 79 cm (39¼ x 31 in.)
San Francisco Museum of Modern Art

She treats the flower grower Luther Burbank as if he were a plant. Through his roots, he is nourished by his own corpse—symbol of the natural cycle, not only in the realm of plants.

3 *Luther Burbank* 1931
Oil on hardboard, 87.6 x 62.2 cm (34½ x 24½ in.)
Dolores Olmedo Foundation, Mexico City

Down to the last detail, the bed is identical to the one Frida was actually born in. Frida, whose mother died while this painting was being made, is giving birth to herself, as she says. The corpse on the bed is both Frida and her mother. "A birth that produced the only woman able to present in her art the feelings, responsibilities, and creative possibilities of women with unsurpassable physical commitment," wrote Diego Rivera.

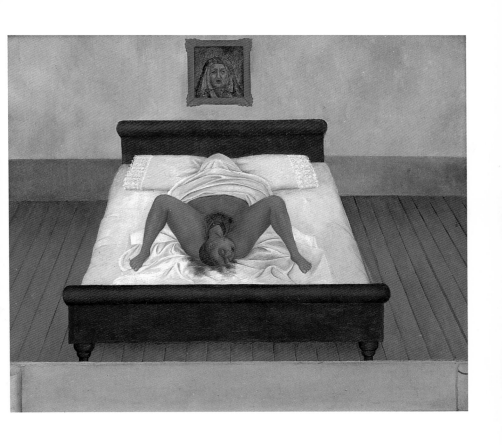

4 *My Birth* *1932*

Oil on metal, 30. 5 x 35. 6 cm (12 x 14 in.)
Private collection, U.S.A.

Frida, who longed to have a child, is lying in a hospital bed in Detroit, where Rivera was working on a mural. She lost the baby after three months of pregnancy. She is surrounded by symbolic objects that are fixed to red bands like umbilical cords and connected to her stomach: illustrations from medical textbooks—Frida originally wanted to become a doctor—such as her pelvis, injured in the accident, and a section through the lower abdomen, an orchid that looks like a removed uterus, a snail that symbolizes the painful slowness of the miscarriage, the dead baby, and the gruesome apparatus used to sterilize surgical instruments. Like Mexican ex-voto paintings, this painting is on metal. The objects resemble the emblems, instruments of torture, and severed limbs seen in religious pictures.

5 Henry Ford Hospital 1932

Oil on metal, 30.5 x 38 cm (12 x 15 in.)
Dolores Olmedo Foundation, Mexico City

In 1935, Diego and Frida separated. Frida could no longer put up with his infidelities, but the separation was very painful for her. In the newspaper, she read a story about a man who killed his lover by stabbing her many times with a knife, and said in court, "I gave her only a few little pricks." Once again, the banner is carried by a pair of doves. The words are taken from a contemporary hit song. Frida was inspired here as well by the work of the popular graphic artist and painter José Guadalupe Posada, who around the turn of the century published news sheets about everyday murders.

6 A Few Little Stabs 1935
Oil on metal, 38 x 48.5 cm (15 x 19 in.) (with frame)
Dolores Olmedo Foundation, Mexico City

In 1939, when Diego was fifty-three and Frida thirty-two, she wrote to him, "My child—the great unknown—it is six in the morning, and the turkeys are singing. Heat of human tenderness. Accompanied solitude. I will never forget your presence all my life. . . . The name Diego: the name of love. Never let the tree grow thirsty that loves you so much, that preserved your seed, that crystallized your life at six in the morning."

7 Portrait of Diego Rivera 1937
Oil on wood, 46 x 32 cm (18 x 12½ in.)
Collection of Jacques and Natasha Gelman, Mexico City

Even among the poor, it is the custom in Mexico for children who have died to be laid out dressed as angels. Later, the body is rolled into a *petate,* a straw mat, and buried in it. Frida has just suffered a miscarriage. On the dead child's pillow lies a religious picture showing a suffering Christ.

8 The Dead Dimas Rosas at the Age of Three 1937

Oil on hardboard, 48 x 31.5 cm (19 x 12½ in.)
Dolores Olmedo Foundation, Mexico City

The Indian wet nurse, wearing an Aztec mask, is an aspect
of Frida herself, the Indian part of her, which gives the weak
European part strength and nourishes it. On the one hand,
it is a depiction of a Madonna, and on the other of an Earth
Mother—Nature as a beneficent, lavish provider of nourish-
ment, who makes milk rain down from the heavens and
whose breasts, like vine stems, are rich with grapes.

9 My Wet Nurse and I 1937

Oil on metal, 30.5 x 34. 7 cm (12 x 13¾ in.)
Dolores Olmedo Foundation, Mexico City

After two years, Frida has still not recovered from her separation from Diego. She stands, lacking arms, between the sea and the land, between a dangling school uniform and the costume of the women of Tijuana, which Diego most liked to see her wearing. Tiny malevolent cupids have driven an iron rod through the space her heart used to occupy and are see-sawing on it. Her heart, gigantic and threatening, is pumping rivers of blood across the landscape.

10 Memory, or the Heart 1937
Oil on metal, 40 x 28 cm (15¾ x 11 in.)
Private collection, Paris

The monkey, Fulang Chang, is tied to Frida's hair with pink ribbons. In Mexico, the monkey symbolized both death and the clown, *el vasilon;* at the same time, the animal is a symbol of vitality, which Frida magically binds to herself. It offers protection against loneliness.

11 Fulang Chang and I 1937

Oil on hardboard, 40 x 28 cm (15¾ x 11 in.)
Museum of Modern Art, New York

The little dog, an *itzcuintli*, one of the famous hairless dogs shown even in pre-Columbian codices, is not live, but an Aztec clay figure. Frida, who is smoking marijuana, has no relationship with the dog. The painting was made after one of her miscarriages.

12 Self-Portrait with Itzcuintli Dog ca. 1938
Oil on canvas, 71 x 52 cm (28 x 20½ in.)
Private collection, Dallas, Texas

13 Self-Portrait with Monkey 1938
Oil on hardboard, 40.6 x 30.5 cm (16 x 12 in.)
Albright-Knox Art Gallery, Buffalo, New York

A little girl in front of the vast, naked mountain range in the background has hidden her face behind a paper death mask of the type that can be bought on every corner during carnival.

14 Girl with Death Mask I 1939
Oil on metal, 19.8 x 14.7 cm (7¾ x 5¾ in.)
Private collection, Monterrey, Mexico

"A hidden materialism," writes Rivera, "is present in the divided hearts, in the blood pouring from the table, in the bath water, the plants, the flowers, and in the artist's arteries, which are closed by vessel clips. . . . Frida's art is collectively individual."

15 Pitahayas 1938

Oil on metal, 27 x 36 cm (10½ x 14 in.)
Madison Art Center, Madison, Wisconsin

16 Fruits of the Earth 1938

Oil on hardboard, 40.6 x 60 cm (16 x 23½ in.)
Banco Nacional de México Collection, Mexico City

17 What the Water Gave Me 1938

Oil on canvas, 91 x 70. 5 cm (36 x 27¼ in.)
Isidore Ducasse Fine Arts Collection, New York

Frida's Indian and Spanish personae are connected by their hands and the circulation of their blood. In the Indian Frida's hand is a small medallion showing Diego as a child. The blood arises from the medallion and is pumped across to the other Frida, who is trying close the artery with a surgical clamp. She has not succeeded. The drops of blood mingle with the flower pattern on her dress.

18 The Two Fridas 1939
Oil on canvas, 173.5 x 173 cm (68¼ x 68 in.)
Museo de Arte Moderno, Mexico City

After her friend's suicide—she jumped from a skyscraper window—Frida painted the event for Dorothy Hale's mother, who was horrified and insisted that the band with information, added to the ex-voto image in the usual way, be painted over.

En la ciudad de [Nueva] York el día 21 del mes de Octubre de 1938, a las seis de la mañana, se suicidó la señora DOROTHY HALE tirándose desde una ventana muy alta del edificio Hampshire House. En su recuerdo, [este] retablo, habiéndolo ejecutado FRIDA KAHLO

19 The Suicide of Dorothy Hale 1939
Oil on hardboard, 60.4 x 48. 6 cm (23¾ x 19 in.) (with frame)
Phoenix Art Museum, Phoenix, Arizona

The bed in which Frida slept, and in which she lay when she was ill, is reproduced here exactly. The large "Judas figure" in the form of a skeleton is one of the famous Mexican fireworks figures, which often take up to half an hour to burn down. The bed is floating, but it carries with it thorny plants that encircle Frida, partly choking her and partly caressing her.

20 *The Dream, or the Bed* 1940

Oil on canvas, 74 x 98.5 cm (29 x 38¾ in.)
Collection of Selma and Nesuhi Ertegun, New York

21 Self-Portrait with Monkey 1940
Oil on hardboard, 55.2 x 43.5 cm (21¾ x 17 in.)
Private collection, U.S.A.

"Look, if I love you, it is for your hair; now you are bald,
I love you no more," ran a verse from a folk song. Diego
loved Frida's hair; when they separated, Frida cut it off.
Pelona, the bald-headed one, was Frida's word for death.
While in the hospital after her accident as a girl, she wrote
in a letter, "Pelona has not got me."

22 *Self-Portrait with Shorn Hair* *1940*

Oil on canvas, 40 x 28 cm (15¾ x 11 in.)
Museum of Modern Art, New York

Frida described the colors on her palette as follows:
    "Green: warm, good light.
    Crimson: Azteca Tlapalli (a Mexican gemstone), old prickly-pear blood. The most lively and the oldest.
    Coffee brown: color of mole (a Mexican sauce, Diego's favorite dish), the dying leaf, earth.
    Yellow: craziness, death, fear, part of the sun and of joy.
    Cobalt blue: electricity and purity, love.
    Black: nothing is black, really nothing.
    Leaf green: leaves, sadness, science; the whole of Germany is this color.
    Greenish yellow: even crazier and more mysterious; the clothes of all ghosts are this color . . . at least their underclothes.
    Dark green: the color of bad advertising and good business.
    Navy blue: distance; also tenderness came from this blueness.
    Red: blood? Ah, who knows?"

23 *Self-Portrait, Dedicated to Sigmund Firestone* 1940

Oil on hardboard, 61 x 43 cm (24 x 17 in.)
Private collection, U.S.A.

24 *Self-Portrait, Dedicated to Dr. Eloesser 1940*
Oil on hardboard, 59.7 x 40 cm (23½ x 15¾ in.)
Private collection, U.S.A.

Frida is wearing a wreath of thorns around her neck, from which a dead hummingbird hangs. In Mexico, the hummingbird is, on the one hand, a talisman for happiness in love and, on the other, the bird dead heroes are reincarnated as when they return to earth. The two pets are not comforting as companions here. The monkey, which is picking at the chain of thorns, is making the torture worse, and the cat has its eye on the hummingbird.

25 *Self-Portrait with Thorny Necklace 1940*

Oil on canvas, 63.5 x 49. 5 cm (25 x 19½ in.), Iconography Collection,
Harry Ransom Humanities Research Center, University of Texas, Austin

26 My Parrots and I 1941
Oil on canvas, 82 x 62.8 cm (32¼ x 24¾ in.)
Private collection, New Orleans, Louisiana

Now that she and Diego have remarried, she depicts herself adorned with the hair she had cut off in sorrow when they separated.

27 Self-Portrait with Plait 1941
Oil on hardboard, 51 x 38. 7 cm (20 x 15¼ in.)
Collection of Jacques and Natasha Gelman, Mexico City

28 Roots, or the Pedregal 1943

Oil on metal, 30.5 x 49.9 cm (12 x 19½ in.)
Private collection, Houston, Texas

29 Self-Portrait with Monkeys 1943
Oil on canvas, 81.5 x 63 cm (32 x 24¾ in.)
Collection of Jacques and Natasha Gelman, Mexico City

30 Thoughts of Death 1943
Oil on canvas, mounted on hardboard, 45 × 36.8 cm (17¾ × 14½ in.)
Dolores Olmedo Foundation, Mexico City

As her health gradually grew weaker and weaker, Frida had to wear a steel jacket for five months. "To hope, to suppress fear, the broken column, the long terrible look, without being able to walk on the broad path . . . to move my life, that is made of steel," she wrote in her diary.

31 *The Broken Column 1944*
Oil on canvas, mounted on hardboard, 40 x 30.7 cm (15¾ x 12 in.)
Dolores Olmedo Foundation, Mexico City

A yellow ribbon links Frida with the monkeys, the pre-Columbian idol from Colima, and the dog, Señor Xólotl, who was named after a god descended from Venus and known as the "wonderful twin." The ribbon also encircles the blood-red signature and a nail that sticks into the clouds in the background.

32 *Self-Portrait with Monkeys* 1945

Oil on hardboard, 56.8 x 41. 3 cm (22¼ x 16¼ in.)
Dolores Olmedo Foundation, Mexico City

Two years after Frida read Freud's book on Moses, she showed her friends for the first time this "mosaic dominated by historical, cultic, and occultist ideas" (as Raquel Tibol described it). In 1945, she had a signed article on the painting published in the Mexican journal *Así*.

"The real theme of the painting is Moses," she wrote, "or, put it better, it is the birth of the hero. But I have generalized the facts and images from the book . . . in my own (very confused) way. What I wanted to bring out particularly distinctly and clearly is that pure fear forces humanity to invent or imagine heroes and gods. Fear of life and fear of death." Alongside Christ, Zarathustra, Alexander, Caesar, Muhammad, Tamburlaine, and Napoleon, Hitler is also depicted.

33 Moses, or the Core of Creation 1945

Oil on hardboard, 75.6 x 61 cm (29¾ x 24 in.)
Private collection, Houston, Texas

Only the easel, riding on the bed, is holding up the horrific conglomeration of fears and death that Frida is both vomiting up and also to an extent being violently force-fed. She lies exposed in the sterile, rocky desert of a Mexican volcanic landscape. She is naked, as if after an operation; after her accident, too, she was left naked, as the crash tore the clothes from her body.

34 *Without Hope* 1945
Oil on canvas, mounted on hardboard, 28 x 36 cm (11 x 14 in.)
Dolores Olmedo Foundation, Mexico City

After yet another back operation in New York, Frida's condition failed to improve. She was in great pain, and had to wear a steel jacket. The "Indian Frida," in a red Tijuana costume, is holding the jacket like an instrument of torture, but also like a trophy, on the flag, the pole of which may be either a paintbrush dipped in red color or a surgical instrument covered in blood. On the flag is written, "Tree of hope, stay strong."

35 Tree of Hope, Stay Strong 1946
Oil on hardboard, 56 x 40.6 cm (22 x 16 in.)
Isidore Ducasse Fine Arts Collection, New York

The hart, injured and felled by arrows, is found traditionally in Mexico in dances, songs, and pictures. Juana Inés de la Cruz (1659—1695) writes in a love poem,

"When you see a wounded hart rushing down a slope
To cool its wounds in an icy river
And falling with thirst into the crystal water:
Not in relief, but in its pain it is my image."

36 The Little Hart 1946

Oil on hardboard, 22.4 x 30 cm (8¾ x 11¾ in.)
Collection of Carolyn Farb, Houston, Texas

Aqui me pinté yo, Frida Kahlo, con
la imágen del espejo. Tengo 37 años,
y es el mes de Julio de mil novecientos
cuarenta y siete. En Coyoacán, México,
lugar donde nací.

37 Self-Portrait with Loose Hair 1947

Oil on hardboard, 61 x 45 cm (24 x 17¾ in.)
Private collection, Mexico City

Frida in the festive costume of the women of Tijuana.
The three tears are the three ritual tears of the Mater Dolor-
osa. It looks as if she is sticking her head through a hole in
one of the painted screens that Mexican photographers set
up at fairs to take snapshots of their customers against what
is for them an exotic, or perhaps elegant, background.

38 Self-Portrait 1948
Oil on hardboard, 48.3 x 39. 3 cm (19 x 15½ in.)
Private collection, Mexico City

The great embrace of the universe encloses the stars, the earth, plants — and Frida, who holds a naked Diego in her lap like a mother holding her baby. During her final years, Frida felt more and more like Diego's mother. "Every moment he is my child," she writes. "My child, which is born every moment, which is born from me every day." But she also writes, "Diego was not and never will be a husband to anybody."

*39 The Loving Embrace of the Universe, the Earth (Mexico),
Diego, Myself, and Señor Xólotl 1949*

Oil on canvas, 70 x 60.5 cm (27½ x 23¾ in.)
Collection of Jorge Contreras Chacel, Mexico City

Frida painted this picture when she was afraid Diego was about to leave her again and marry Maria Felix, a celebrated film star and close friend of Frida's.

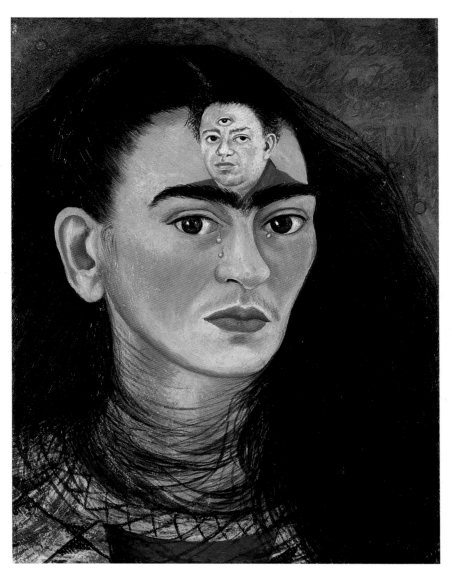

40 Diego and I 1949
Oil on canvas, mounted on hardboard, 29.5 x 22.4 cm (11½ x 8¾ in.)
Collection of Mary-Anne Martin/Fine Arts, New York

"Dr. Farrill saved me, he gave me back my joy in life," writes Frida in her diary after her last operation. "I want to live. I have already started painting."

In 1950 and 1951, Frida had to undergo seven operations on her spine.

41 *Self-Portrait with Portrait of Dr. Farrill 1951*
Oil on hardboard, 42 x 50 cm (16½ x 19¾ in.)
Private Collection, Mexico City

The Mexican still life, with sliced and decorated fruit, was a traditional subject in the colonial period and in primitive painting, as in advertising billboards and fruit-juice stands in the marketplace.

42 Fruit of Life 1953

Oil on hardboard, 47 x 62 cm (18½ x 24½ in.)
Private collection, Mexico City

43 Viva la vida (Long Live Life) 1954

Oil on hardboard, 52 x 72 cm (20½ x 28¼ in.)
Frida Kahlo Museum, Mexico City

Chronology

1907 On July 6, Magdalena Carmen Frieda [*sic*] Kahlo is born in Coyoacán, a suburb of Mexico City, as the third daughter of the photographer Guillermo Kahlo and his wife, Matilde. Her father, originally named Wilhelm, was born in Germany of Hungarian immigrants, and emigrated to Mexico in 1891; her mother was a Mexican. Frida Kahlo later gives 1910, the year of the Mexican revolution , as her year of birth. The Blue House, in which she was born and which she lived in—at times together with Diego Rivera—and used as a studio, is now the Museo Frida Kahlo.

1913 She is confined to bed for several months with polio. The illness causes permanent crookedness in her right foot.

1923 Commences high school at the Escuela Nacional Preparatoria.

1925 Takes graphic art lessons with the artist Fernando Fernandéz, is much occupied with painting, and watches Diego Rivera paint the mural *Creation* at her school. On September 17, she is so seriously injured in a traffic accident that she will remain handicapped and in constant pain for the rest of her life. Numerous operations, extended hospital stays, months spent in steel and plaster jackets, several miscarriages, and the late amputation of her right leg result from the accident, which ultimately causes her death.

1926 During her convalescence, she begins to draw and paint.

1927 Meets Diego Rivera again, who had been staying in Europe for an extended period.

1928 Meets the photographer Tina Modotti, through her comes into contact with left-wing intellectual figures from literature and politics, and joins the Communist Party.

1929 In August, Diego Rivera and Frida Kahlo marry; he is forty-two and she twenty-two. They are to remain childless.

1930 First miscarriage. In November, Frida Kahlo and Diego Rivera travel to

San Francisco. They spend four years in the U.S.A., apart from four short interruptions. In San Francisco, she meets the American photographer Edward Weston and Dr. Leo Eloesser, whose patient she becomes during the following years.

1931 Meets the Russian film director Sergei Eisenstein in Mexico City.

1932 Frida and Diego Rivera spend several months in Detroit. Frida Kahlo's mother dies on September 15.

1933 Rivera completes murals in Detroit and New York. In December, the couple return to Mexico City, and in 1934 move into a modern duplex house in the suburb of San Angel (now the Museo Casa Rivera).

1935 Separates from Rivera on the grounds of his numerous affairs, including one with her sister Cristina, and travels to New York for several weeks.

1937 In January, Leon Trotsky and his wife, Natalia, come to Mexico. Initially, they stay in the Blue House, in Coyoacán.

1938 André Breton meets Frida Kahlo during a stay in Mexico, and discovers her as a "surrealist." October 25—November 14: her first individual exhibition, in the Julien Levy Gallery in New York. It is an immense success: she sells paintings for the first time. Meets the American photographer Nickolas Muray.

1939 Travels to Europe. In Paris, she is welcomed enthusiastically by the surrealists. Marcel Duchamp arranges for an exhibition of her paintings in the Galerie Renou & Colle. On November 6, Rivera and Kahlo are divorced.

1940 Participates in the International Surrealist Exhibition in Mexico City and in the massive exhibition "Twenty Centuries of Mexican Art" in New York. On August 21, Leon Trotsky is assassinated in Mexico. Frida Kahlo trravels to San Francisco to consult Dr. Eloesser, partly because of increasing alcohol problems. On December 8, Frida Kahlo and Diego Rivera marry in San Francisco for the second time.

1941 Her father dies on April 14. She returns to Mexico.

1943 Teaches at the college for painters and sculptors, La Esmeralda. Soon the lessons are held at the Blue House. Among her students, one group—Los Fridos—makes a name for itself.

1946 The Mexican Education Ministry awards her painting *Moses* a second prize and a government grant.

1950 One-year hospital stay in Mexico City.

1953 First individual exhibition in Mexico, in the Galeria Arte Contemporaneo. Seriously ill, she takes part in the opening while lying in her four-poster bed. April 27: amputation of her right leg.

1954 On April 2, she takes part in a demonstration for Guatemala in her wheelchair. Frida Kahlo dies on July 13 in the Blue House, at the age of forty-seven.

1957 Diego Rivera dies on November 24.

1958 July 30: opening of the Frida Kahlo Museum in the Blue House, in Coyoacán.

Bibliography

Billeter, Erika, ed. *Imagén de México—Der Beitrag Mexikos zur Kunst des 20. Jahrhunderts* (Mexico's contribution to twentieth-century art). Frankfurt am Main: Kunsthalle Schirn, 1987. Catalog of the exhibition in the Kunsthalle Schirn, Frankfurt, and in the Messepalast, Vienna, 1987–88.

Breton, André. *Surrealism and Painting.* Trans. Simon Watson Taylor. New York: Harper and Row, 1972.

Frida Kahlo and Tina Modotti. London: Whitechapel Art Gallery, 1982. Catalog of the 1982 exhibition in London's Whitchapel Art Gallery, with articles by Laura Mulvey, Peter Wollen, André Breton, Diego Rivera, and Alejandro Gómez Arias.

Herrera, Hayden. *Frida: A Biography of Frida Kahlo.* New York: HarperCollins, 1991.

———. *Frida Kahlo: The Paintings.* New York: HarperCollins, 1991.

Lowe, Sarah M. *Frida Kahlo.* New York: Universe, 1991.

Prignitz-Poda, Helga, Salomón Grimberg, and Andrea Kettenmann, eds. *Frida Kahlo: Das Gesamtwerk.* Frankfurt am Main: Verlag Neue Kritik, 1988.

Tibol, Raquel. *Frida Kahlo: An Open Life.* Trans. Elinor Randall. Albuquerque: University of New Mexico Press, 1993.

Zamora, Martha. *Frida Kahlo: The Brush of Anguish.* Trans. Marilyn S. Smith. San Francisco: Chronicle Books, 1990.

Credits for Illustrations